T0131983

EIGHT MONTHS
A LIFETIME

When Trisomy 18 Calls

BELINDA ANN HOGANS PENN EVANS (MEMA)

To order additional copies of this book, contact:
Xlibris
844-714-8691
www.Xlibris.com
Orders@Xlibris.com

ISBN: Softcover 978-1-6641-7595-2
       EBook   978-1-6641-7594-5

Print information available on the last page

Rev. date: 05/20/2021

EIGHT MONTHS
A LIFETIME

When Trisomy 18 Calls

In Loving Memory of Ja'Ciara B'Ann Jefferson (Cia)

Table of Contents

Cia's Entrance

So, when the physicians informed me, they had to perform an emergency C-section, I was shocked. They continued on to say that the umbilical cord was wrapped around the baby's neck, and her heart rate was dropping quickly. They also began to test for any brain damage and other complications that might have occurred. After the testing was complete, my granddaughter Ja'Ciara was immediately medevacked to Shand's Children Hospital in Gainesville, Florida, on her date of birth.

Isn't it funny how we take the simple pleasures of life, and even life itself, for granted? Naively, we think we will have time to enjoy life on another day, all the while we know that tomorrow is not promised.

But be encouraged. I want to take you on my journey with my granddaughter, Ja'Ciara B'Ann Jefferson (Cia). As her grandmother, MeMa, my experience of Cia has been life changing for me. It is my desire to encourage you as you face one of the most trying times in your life, the terminal illness of a child.

Cia was born April 7, 2001, and she is the first born of my daughter, NaTisha. NaTisha's pregnancy took its normal course with doctor visits and preparing the nursery with all the softness of a newborn. Family and friends engaged in the festivities as well. The excitement would culminate with Cia's arrival, but her arrival would not be ushered in the healthy way of most newborns but rather with a terminal illness. I arrived from Atlanta on Thursday in time to accompany my daughter to Tallahassee Memorial Hospital for Cia's birth. On the day of Cia's birth, the physicians informed NaTisha that they had to perform an emergency C-section. She was in shock, and so was I. Complications caused by the umbilical cord wrapped around the baby's neck and her rapidly dropping heart rate necessitated a quick C-section procedure. As I approached the delivery window, the gravity of the situation weighed heavily on my heart. As soon as I peered in the window the nurses closed the curtain to prevent me from seeing what was happening.

"What is wrong?" was my internal cry.

Shortly after, the medical personnel came and told us what they had to do. There was a hole in her heart, and she needed to get to the children's hospital in Gainesville, Florida, about 150 miles away. They were preparing the Medivac Helicopter to transport her as soon as possible.

"I'm going with my baby!" NaTisha said as she hurriedly dressed.

Upon signing release papers for Cia's discharge, we drove to Gainesville. Cia's father, Will, and his mother accompanied us. Coco and another family friend trailed behind us, and we arrived in Gainesville late that night.

Cia was placed in an incubator in the neonatal ward upon arrival At the new hospital, and doctors ran more tests. The doctors later came to inform us what was happening.

I recall sitting around a large conference table next to my daughter with a team of five doctors and specialists waiting, waiting to hear Cia's diagnosis. With hesitation, one of the doctors said,

"Your daughter has a terminal illness known as **Trisomy 18.**"

"What is that?!" NaTisha screamed.

Their reply:

Trisomy 18 is a genetic disorder in which an infant has a third copy of material from chromosome 18, instead of the usual two copies. Trisomy 18 occurs in one of every 6,000 live births. It is three times more common in

girls than boys. The syndrome occurs when there is extra material from chromosome 18. The extra material affects normal development. Infant weight is 4.5 pounds (tiny), although born as a full-term baby. Usually, no signs occur prior to birth to indicate that there is a problem.

The pregnancy was normal, according to the doctors. Problems were not detected until after Cia was born. In addition to the hole in her heart, she had Downs Syndrome in her hands, which was emphasized by the abnormality of her fingers. More specifically, Cia was expected to have only one month to live. If by chance she survived that month, she would not live longer than a year.

We were still reeling from the shock, when the doctors proceeded to offer an option. In situations like this, families are offered an option to leave their terminally ill infants in the care of the Children's Hospital. We were asked if we wanted to proceed with that choice.

NaTisha, holding my hand, squeezed it tightly, andas she looked around the room, her eyes focused intently on each doctor and specialist.

"No Thank You!" The words floated from her heart with firm resolve. "My mother has decorated my baby's room. Cia has a beautiful room. It is waiting for her arrival. She has parents and grandparents who are waiting to give her all the love, care, and support she will ever need. My baby is going home with me."

The doctors and specialists, with all their medical knowledge and expertise, tried to dissuade her by telling NaTisha that that caring for Cia would be extremely difficult and requiring 24/7 care.

"We, my family and I, stand ready to do whatever it takes to care for my daughter as long as she lives," NaTisha replied.

NaTisha was able to hold her daughter for the first time, three days after her birth, when she was taken off the machines. She held Cia close rocking, singing, and caressing her with great care and love. We were able to visit also, but only one person at a time.

The Ronald McDonald House was truly a haven for rest and sleeping, which they provided for us for two weeks. Surgery to repair the hole in Cia's heart was not an option, because the doctors didn't believe she would survive the surgery. Nor did they believe surgery would prolong her life. She was so small. With that said, Cia left the hospital (insert how many days) after her birth.

Cia's Life at Home

NaTisha did extensive research to locate resources that would and could provide and assist with meeting Cia's needs and care. She reduced her work hours to part-time while maintaining health care coverage for her. Will, was also intimately involved in his daughter's life. He continued to work full-time in support of Cia's financial wellbeing and engaged in her overall care as well.

My years of experience in early childhood development were an added help for my granddaughter. And Will's father's experience as a paramedic was also a valued asset.

The families of both parents provided scheduled, daily care for Cia while they worked or needed rest time. This truly was a family affair. I took off a couple of months to get NaTisha and Cia settled. Family members rotated time to spend with Cia. Her daily routine also included home visits from the pediatric nurse, musical therapist, and an occupational therapist.

Cia enjoyed bath time, and it was one of my favorite times with her. I recall my daughter laughingly saying to me that I would bathe all the oil off her skin if I kept it up. Cia was blessed with many clothes. I always wanted to see her well-dressed. When Cia became tired of being held, she became restless. Then it was time to lie down and listen to music. This led to another of my favorite times with her, when I sang to her. Her favorite song was "You Are My Sunshine," and her favorite nursery rhyme was "This Little Piggy." Cia would hold my hand with her tiny fingers during those times, for me only. None of our other family members could get her to do this, not mother nor father.

Trips were planned for Cia to ensure that grandparents, uncles, aunts, and nieces could spend with her. The doctors had given us the green light to do as much as we could with her because time was short. Given the green light meant that I had to share Cia with others. I felt a little selfish about that. I didn't really want to share her, but I did. And I am so very glad, because we all were able to have our own special memories of the time we had with her.

Road trips were organized to provide enough time to stop along the way for Cia to rest, move around, get massaged, and enjoy the outside. So, driving a usually five-hour trip might take eight to nine hours. Between trips, Cia was given time to rest with her mom and dad.

Cia's road trips included:

- Jacksonville, Florida: Spent time with Will's family andCia's grandfather for a week
- Tallahassee, Florida: Home visits with her Will's mother, Cia's grandmother
- Atlanta, Georgia: with me, MeMa, Cia's maternal grandmother
- Mexico Beach, Panama City, Florida: Kia's "Wet Day" with MeMa and Ann
- Panama City, Florida: A visit Cia's great aunt, Gwen
- Vero Beach, Florida: Visit with Cia's Uncle, Clifton, in prison

NaTisha's father, Penn, came from Ft. Walton, Florida, to spend several days with Cia. She was always surrounded by family and friends. Cia was LOVED by all.

Cia's Wet Day

with MeMa

I desperately wished for "Cia" to see the ocean. So, on the first weekend in September, when Cia was just at five-months-old, we loaded up the car and headed to Mexico Beach, Panama City Beach, Florida. My cousin, Ann (Cia's great aunt), joined us for the ride. Cia was well-dressed for the occasion, dolled up in a one-piece swimsuit for "preemies." On the way, I began to thank God for allowing me the opportunity to enjoy this time with my granddaughter. I apologized to God for taking for granted the gifts He gives us to enjoy daily.

As we strolled across beach searching for the exact spot to unfold the beach blanket and pop up the umbrella, Cia became the main attraction. People could hardly believe there was a bathing suit and sunglasses on such a tiny baby. I brought along all the necessary appropriate equipment for fun in the sun. The first thing I did was to lay down a beach towel and set up an umbrella for shade. Next, my cousin Ann and I began to take pictures one after another. What a photo shoot it was!

The weather was clear and sunny. The tide was relatively low, and you could hear the air whisper across the water. Cia and I sat on the slightly moistened, cool sand. Gently, I rubbed her hands across the gritty sand; so that she could get acquainted with the texture. I soon noticed her wiggling her toes in the sand. With a bucket in one hand, I held Cia close to my chest as we walked along the edge of the ocean collecting seashells and silver dollars in the sand. Cia showed fascination with the seashell colors and shapes as I held each before her eyes. I placed a seashell to her ear, hoping she could hear the gentle echoes of the ocean's waves.

Time to get wet! As I held her in my arms, we slowly walked into the water. At first, she quickly jerked her feet

Away from the water, but then her tiny body slowly adjusted to the water's temperature. Within minutes in the water, Cia looked in awe at the water surging back and forth. Because of all the rippling of the waves, no one thing held her attention for too long. She occasionally looked at the children playing on the beach and in the water. She gazed at those walking by who stopped to acknowledge her beauty. Suddenly, Cia's feet jerked again. She clenched my hands, and her eyes widened like a full moon, as the water had tickled her feet once more. Ann and I laughed at Cia's reaction to the feel of water beneath her feet. Cia's experiences and reactions at the ocean's beach was all that I had hoped and more.

Ann reached to hold Cia. Slowly, Ann began to caress Cia body ever so gently in the water. Then, unexpectantly, Cia licked Ann's hand while looking up at me. I carefully lowered my body to sit at edge of the water, securely, and I reached for Cia. Holding her in my lap, allowing the water to splash onto us both. Again, her feet jerked, and her eyes widened as a full moon. This was Cia's "Wet Day!" This was my joy as her MeMa!

Once, we got out of the water, I sat in the sand, with Cia in my lap, and began to build a sandcastle. Some of the children on the beach came over to help. But they were really more interested in Cia. "She is so tiny, like a baby doll," some of the children remarked.

They even asked if they could holder her. I found it difficult to explain Cia's condition, and at the same time, I didn't want to disappoint them by not allowing them to hold her. So, I began by explaining the seriousness of Cia's illness and how very fragile she was. Then, under my strict supervision, I decided to allow them to hold her. I don't know who felt more rewarded, the children or me, perhaps.

As evening approached, we began to pack up, fold the blanket, and let down the umbrella. We prepared Cia to say goodbye to the beach, to say goodbye to her "Wet Day." Later, I sat with my granddaughter on the deck of a restaurant and watched shades of pink and orange light the sky. While gazing upon the sunset, the atmosphere was so peaceful and relaxing that before I realized it, Cia was fast asleep.

This had been a dream come true as we shared the precious moments of time and experienced what so many of us take for granted – living in the moment and basking in the beauty and sensations of God's creation.

Cia's Christmas in November

It was a tradition in the Hogans household to decorate for Christmas on the Friday after Thanksgiving. I grew up knowing that my father would find a tree in the woods on his mother's land. We listened to Christmas music, strung popcorn, and made icicles out of aluminum foil. Any ideas we had turned into the decorations. It was so much fun.

When I got married, it became the Penn family's Thanksgiving tradition to set up the Christmas tree on the day after Thanksgiving. It had begun with my father and mother, Nokomis and Lizzie Mae. Now, I had carried the tradition into my family. NaTisha had experienced the excitement of this holiday tradition since her childhood as well.

This year though, in 2001, after Thanksgiving dinner, we gathered in the living room near the fireplace and listened to "Motown Christmas." A sense of urgency flowed through me. I realized it had been seven months, and Cia was still with us. As we drew closer to the completion of a year of her life, I knew that time was short.

Cia had lived longer than expected. She did things that were not expected. She was able to raise her hand, look around, and smile. She moved her feet and legs, turned head from side to side, and looked at us with engaging eyes. Cia responded to touches, and she loved music for relaxing.

I thought about Cia's first Christmas. Would she be with us that far into December? I didn't know. But I knew that I wanted her to feel the joys of family at Christmas time. So, we decided to celebrate Christmas in November with and for Cia. However, the excitement of purchasing gifts and sharing Christmas with Cia began in October.

A natural tree was one of the many things on my Wish List to Santa for Cia's first Christmas and the only thing left to be done. I indulged her in a conversation about the Christmas Tree, as she smack her lips and ate small portions of liquid from collard greens mixed with corn bread – one of the many dishes that was prepared for Thanksgiving dinner.

The Penn family tradition was to put up the Christmas Tree after Thanksgiving dinner. My daughter, in tune to my conversation with my granddaughter, rose up from lying on the sofa.

"Mom, today being the day after Thanksgiving – if we purchase a tree – I don't know if it will stay green for Christmas," she said. "But if that is what you want to do, I will purchase a tree."

And with that being said, she was out the door. After her departure, I eagerly rearranged the living room furniture, moving a chair that sat by the fireplace, to make room for the perfect place for the natural tree. Carefully, removing boxes labelled as Christmas decorations from the hall closet, I was interrupted by the soul stirring and soulful sound of the Temptations singing "Merry Christmas," and then Maze singing "Back in Stride Again."

I lifted Cia from her swing, held her in my arms with her cheek gently touching my cheek, and we began to twist, turn, rock, and sway from side to side to the joyous sound of the music, occasionally stopping to exchange smiles.

The rumbling sounds of keys and the turning of the doorknob interrupted our dance. As I ran to the door, it flung open, and to my surprise there stood a huge six-foot, pear-shaped Balsamic Christmas tree. After several minutes of pushing and turning the tree, NaTisha was able to get the tree in the house.

"Mom, I hope the tree is large enough for you, because it sure did cost enough," NaTisha said, exhausted.

We laughed while Cia sat quietly in her swing moving forward and backward as she watched her mom and MeMa trim the lower branches to fit the tree into the stand. She watched as we strung the lights and hung the bulbs on the tree. From the excitement, Cia became restless. I took her from the swing and comforted her as her mother continued to hang bulbs on the tree and stockings by the fireplace. Presents were place under the tree.

NaTisha, and I sat with Cia by the Christmas tree, and watched as her eyes moved in the directions of the sparkling lights and dancing ornaments. Oh, what a joyous time!

Cia's Message

We never talked about her dying.

We purchased a special chair to help her sit up, styled like a walker to support her back and neck. She loved being in the swinger. Cia's muscle mass never allowed her to hold her bottle. She struggled to raise her hand to get it kissed by me. I was always in her face. I had to make sure she was able to make bowel movements and pass gas, or she would get in a frightful mood. I gently rubbed and massaged her to help. A bowel movement is so much harder to do without the muscle mass to push it out. Sometimes, enemas were needed. I felt like it was hurting her, and I couldn't handle it. So, Mama NaTisha had to do that part.

Ja'Ciara delivered a message to her family. The message was: "LOVE. TIME IS PRECIOUS. LIFE IS A STRUGGLE. Give yourself to God completely, and you will win."

I often wonder if Cia had not been born with such a severe illness, would I have felt the sense of urgency to enjoy things like the beach, or watching the sunset with her. I cannot say for sure, but there is one thing my beautiful granddaughter taught me that is precious: relationships are important, and they should be handled carefully.

Ja Ciara B'Ann Jefferson ascended to heaven with her creator on December 7, 2001. She lived exactly eight months, and I am grateful and very blessed that we shared a relationship like none other in my lifetime. I have kept the seashells and will forever enjoy the memories of that day at the beach.

Most importantly, I enjoyed sharing a small part of her life and mine with you on this journey. Cia's life touched my life in a very special way and changed me forever... Just as we prepare mentally and physically for our children entering into adult hood; so must we also prepare for their death. For me, personally, I found myself grasping for every opportunity to be active in her life. It was important that she knew both my voice and my scent. There is no doubt in my mind that she knew exactly who I was and how very much I loved her. The bond grandparents share with their grandchildren is as enduring and passionate as the one shared with their own children. At least it has proven to be so for me.

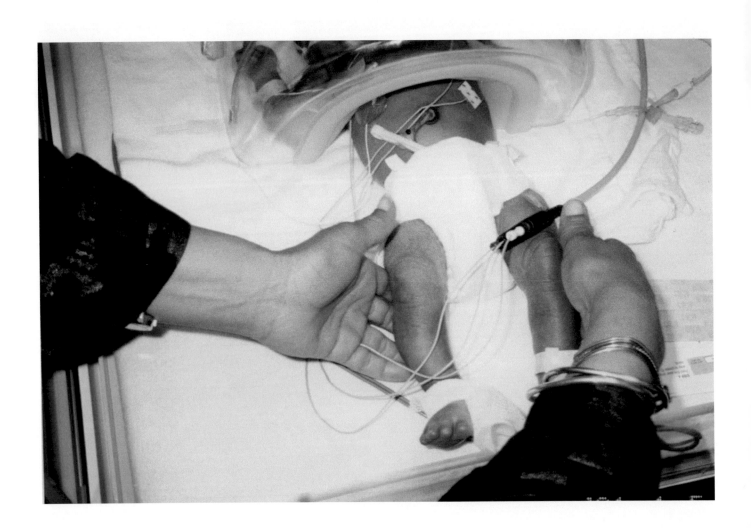

Printed in the United States
by Baker & Taylor Publisher Services